A Beginner's Guide to Releasing Trapped Emotions

Going Deeper, Book 1

Chariss K. Walker

Disclaimer

Although the author and publisher have made every effort to ensure that the information in this book was correct at press time, the author and publisher do not assume and hereby disclaim any liability to any party for any loss, damage, or disruption caused by errors or omissions, whether such errors or omissions result from negligence, accident, or any other cause. Because of the dynamic nature of the Internet, any Web addresses or links contained in this book may have changed since this publication and may no longer be valid.

The author's intent is to offer information of a general nature that will help you, the reader, in your search for spiritual well-being. The author does not dispense medical advice or prescribe medications of any kind. This book is not intended as a substitute for the medical advice of physicians. The reader should regularly consult a physician in matters relating to his/her health and particularly with respect to any symptoms that may require diagnosis or medical attention.

For Wholesale and Library Distribution:
Create Space Direct
Attn: Customer Service
4900 Lacross Road
N. Charleston, SC 29406
Fax: (206) 922-5928
Email: info@createspace.com
Website: https://www.createspace.com

Libraries and booksellers interested in stocking The Journey and other books by Chariss K. Walker --

Direct Reseller Application --
https://www.createspace.com/pub/l/createspacedirect.do

A Beginner's Guide to Releasing Trapped Emotions

Table of Contents

If you don't think your anxiety, depression, sadness and stress impact our physical health, think again. All of these emotions trigger chemical reactions in your body, which can lead to inflammation and a weakened immune system. Learn to cope, sweet friend. There will always be dark days. —Kris Carr

Life experience brings out different emotions and different perspectives on things. I just want to be constantly evolving. —Kiesza

Your intellect may be confused, but your emotions will never lie to you. —Roger Ebert

If you want to have a life that is worth living, a life that expresses your deepest feelings and emotions and cares and dreams, you have to fight for it.
—Alice Walker

Negative emotions like loneliness, envy, and guilt have an important role to play in a happy life; they're big, flashing signs that something need to change.
—Gretchen Rubin

What you believe is very powerful. If you have toxic emotions of fear, guilt, and depression, it is because you have wrong thinking because of wrong believing.
—Joseph Prince

You need to put what you learn into practice and do it over and over again until it's a habit. I always say, 'Seeing in not believing. Doing is believing.' There is a lot to learn about fitness, nutrition, and emotions, but once you do, you can master them instead of them mastering you. —Brett Hoebel

We cannot selectively numb emotions; when we numb the painful emotions, we also numb the positive emotions. —Brené Brown

Gratitude is the healthiest of all human emotions. The more you express gratitude for what you have, the more likely you will have even more to express gratitude for.
—Zig Ziglar

Not only do happy people endure pain better and take more health and safety precautions when threatened, but positive emotions undo negative emotions.
—Martin Seligman

Just as your car runs more smoothly and requires less energy to go faster and farther when the wheels are in perfect alignment, you perform better when your thoughts, feelings, emotions, goals, and values are in balance. —Brian Tracy

If you're self-compassionate, you'll tend to have higher self-esteem than if you're endlessly self-critical. And like high self-esteem, self-compassion is associated with significantly less anxiety and depression, as well as more happiness, optimism, and positive emotions.
—David D. Burns

If your emotional abilities aren't in hand, if you don't have self-awareness, if you are not able to manage your distressing emotions, if you can't have empathy and have effective relationships, then no matter how smart you are, you are not going to get very far.
—Daniel Goleman

So the first step in seeking happiness is learning. We first have to learn how negative emotions and behaviors are harmful to us and how positive emotions are helpful. —Dalai Lama

Strong emotions such as passion and bliss are indications that you're connected to Spirit, or 'inspired,' if you will. When you're inspired, you activate dormant forces, and the abundance you seek in any form comes streaming into your life. —Wayne Dyer

Introduction

**The first and simplest emotion which we discover in the
human mind is curiosity.
~~ Edmund Burke**

In this book, you won't need any special tools other than the power
of your mind – in other words, you must be able to visualize or see
clearly the instructions given. If you have trouble visualizing or if you
are unfamiliar with how to visualize, I recommend that you read my
book, *A Beginner's Guide to Visualization: Tips to See Clearly*
by Chariss K. Walker [2018, ISBN: 978-1986634397] available in
eBook and paperback, before you begin this course. You will also
need to be proficient at Applied Kinesiology or what is commonly
called muscle testing. Don't worry. I have given detailed instructions
for that.

This series of books is written for those who desire to release their
trapped emotions (emotionally charged events from your past) in
several areas whether your body, your mind, or your soul. Those
emotionally charged events are known to inhibit your personal and
spiritual growth, your health and wellness, and your overall fitness in
society. This is the first book in a 6-book series, *Going Deeper*. In this
series, each book includes the same first two chapters, Muscle
Testing and Digging up Trapped Emotions. After you have
completed this book, you can select any of the books in any order of
the series.

The books are listed below and each one takes you a little deeper in your self-healing process. After you have read this book and completed the work, you can choose to release many more trapped emotions in many other areas. Pick all of them, or pick and choose which ones you desire to work on next.

- A Beginner's Guide to Releasing Trapped Emotions (Going Deeper, Book 1)
- Release Chakra Trapped Emotions (Going Deeper, Book 2)
- Release Common Disease Trapped Emotions (Going Deeper, Book 3)
- Release Hindrances to Success Trapped Emotions (Going Deeper, Book 4)
- Release Body System Trapped Emotions, (Going Deeper, Book 5)
- Release Mental Blocks, (Going Deeper, Book 6)

As a Reiki Master/Teacher, I believe that every physical, mental, and spiritual ailment begins with a trapped emotion. With that knowledge I began to release my trapped emotions. I read a lot of books; I went to a lot of practitioners who promised to help. In the end, I did the work myself. After I worked on releasing my emotionally charged events from the past, a new understanding opened for me. New pathways were revealed so that I could use that new information to go further in my self-healing process.

Self-healing work is a lot like peeling an onion, and I refer to that often in this series because it is so true. There is another level where we can go deeper. I found more areas to release trapped emotions. For example, I released trapped emotions and mental blocks in my body systems, my chakras, as well as my mind and soul. The work was amazing and I saw tremendous benefits from it.

Now, I share that information with you.

If you are reading the eBook version, you will need a notebook and pen for the exercises presented in this book. You will use the notebook to record your trapped emotions when you find them as you work through each trapped emotion (TEs) listed in this book. If you are reading the paperback version, I have allowed ample extra pages for your notes; however, you might also like to use a notebook. I keep a notebook to record all the trapped emotions I find, the date I find them, and the date they are released.

On occasion, I return to the list to see if a trapped emotion has returned. It doesn't happen often, but it can happen because we are only human. If the event that caused the original TE returns, we **can** allow that feeling to become trapped again... especially if we haven't changed our reaction to the emotion. Releasing that TE promptly is important. You might wonder how a released trapped emotion can return... I'm going to be repetitive here: We might release the trapped emotions, but we don't always change our attitudes, feelings, or habits about a particular situation. We haven't learned to act or respond to the situation in a new way; we simply react the same old way allowing the emotion to become trapped once again.

I am not a medical professional, but I am what some would call a 'healer' who has studied many metaphysical techniques in order to attain personal and spiritual growth. I have gathered this information from many years of study and earning educational degrees. I have researched, studied resources, and meditated in order to compile this information so that I could use it to release my own trapped emotions and mental blocks. As I now share it with you, my hope is that you will benefit from the material as much as I have.

If I have made any mistakes in any of the chapters, whether content or spelling, I know you will be forgiving of that rather than take exception to it. Intention is the "key" to this work. In organizing this material for this series of books, it was tedious and a massive undertaking, but my desire to share it with you propelled me on.

Perhaps you have already worked with other release methods such as *The Emotion Code* by Dr. Bradley Nelson, [2007, ISBN: 978-

0979553707] or Larry Crane's *The Release Technique Course* [1998. **ISBN-13:** 978-0971175501] or *Many Paths to Healing* by Chariss K. Walker, [2016, ISBN: 978-1530942107]. If so, then you are familiar with release techniques.

As I publish this book, I noticed another technique which has gained recent popularity, but other than the name, *The Sedona Method* by Hale Dwoskin [2003, ISBN: 978-0971933415], I am not familiar with the work. If you have read or used any of those books/methods, then you are familiar with the terminology and principle of releasing emotions that can get trapped in our bodies, minds, and souls causing undue harm.

I do not know what paths you have taken to get to this stage in your life or to my books on self-healing, however, with that in mind, we will start with the basics that you will need in order to benefit from this book:

1. Muscle Testing (Applied Kinesiology)
2. Digging up Trapped Emotions, a simple release technique that I use and will teach you to use.

If you already know how to muscle test, you can skip that part. And, if you have already learned a release technique, you can also skip that part. The importance of this book for you will be the additional steps to release even more TEs. For those who do not know, I will describe each of the methods I use. Also, keep in mind, there are many YouTube videos that teach muscle testing. Please learn everything you can about the technique and become proficient in its use before you attempt this work

Your Notes:

Your Notes:

Your Notes:

Your Notes:

1 | Muscle testing (Applied Kinesiology)

The purpose of kinesiology is to bypass the limitations of the intellect. ~~ Dr. David R. Hawkins

Skeptics and critics abound regarding Applied Kinesiology or muscle testing. I have met people who hated the idea of muscle testing because someone used the technique on them as a lie-detector test. This is a misuse of the skill and certainly not the purpose of muscle testing, but there are always people who will abuse their power and understanding. We cannot let a few spoil the benefits for many.

As we work with this technique and as we work with releasing all spiritual and emotional ailments, the primary purpose of all healing work is – to do no harm to ourselves or others. In spite of the negative ideas and thoughts about muscle testing, when used as a personal tool, it's a very beneficial and positive aid to self-healing.

Keep in mind that, 20 years ago, the medical profession scoffed at homeopathic doctors. Fifty years ago, they also criticized chiropractors as quacks. Today, both practices have gained respect and followers. It might also help us to remember that, 200 years ago, bloodletting was still a popular medical treatment. It was used for any-and-all illnesses. It had been around and accepted for thousands of years. Medical practitioners doggedly held onto the treatment even though it killed more people than it cured. Bloodletting finally was discredited and discontinued in the late 1800s. Ironically, George Washington might have survived the sore throat that killed him if he hadn't requested his physician to "bleed him."

Suffice it to say, anything new or different causes a certain degree of skepticism, doubting, and ridicule. That could explain negative reactions to the introduction of Traditional Chinese medicine or Eastern Medicine. Acupuncture, acupressure, herbal remedies, and other beneficial treatments have been successfully used for an estimated 5,000 years. Even though they are new to us in the west, they are certainly not new treatments.

With an open mind, we realize that not everything new or recently introduced should be greeted with cynicism or disbelief.

The release of trapped emotions is also a new concept. It requires that we become familiar with muscle testing which is a necessary tool that aids in that technique. It's that simple. We need to be able to muscle test in order to find true and false answers to the statements we will make. Muscle testing is the common term for *applied kinesiology*. It is a technique in alternative medicine that uses the strength of muscles in the diagnosis and treatment of disease and disorders. The illness is either physical, mental, spiritual, or any combination of the three.

The guiding principles in muscle testing:

- When something is good for us (true), the muscles remain strong.

- When something is bad for us (false), the muscles become weak.

A holistic doctor might have you hold a supplement at the center of your chest. Then, he might test the strength of the muscles in your dominant arm – as you hold your arm out, he would press down on the arm to see if it remains strong or if it is weak and easily goes down when pressure is applied. If the arm is weak, the supplement is not beneficial for you or not the one you need. If the arm is strong, it indicates that the supplement would be beneficial to you. He might test several supplements in this way to determine what your body needs most.

There's always a splinter group that will give any idea a bad name by misusing it. We should approach muscle testing with a degree of reverence and exercise caution.

As I've already stated – Muscle Testing in not a human lie-detector and should not be used as such. Anyone who learns the method as a means to discredit others and put them down misuses the gift. As in all healing techniques, whether traditional, alternative, or self-directed, the directive is clear—do no harm.

The purpose of Muscle Testing is to discover Yes/True or No/False answers that assist our personal healing and wellbeing.

It is important to ask permission to muscle test. For example, before testing, we might say, "I have permission to test this situation." Only proceed if you receive a positive or true response. As you work with the technique, you will know that you're usually allowed to test yourself and most family members with regard to their health and healing. It's also important to note that we can be denied permission to test for the following reasons:

- We have personal attachment or expectations regarding the answer.

- Our intentions regarding the information are negative.

- We're not spiritually, mentally, or physically ready to hear the answer at this time.

- We're attempting to invade another's privacy or free will.

- The answer to the statement is none of our business.

- We do not have the person's permission to request the information.

- The person's higher self would not want us to access the information.

- The answer could be misused in some way.

- The answer is harmful in some way.

- We're not yet allowed to know the information.

- The answer does not serve the highest good of all those present or concerned.

- The statement/question is not directed in a manner that true or false is an adequate answer.

The body never lies. ~~ Martha Graham

How to Muscle Test Using the Hands:

First, with your non-dominant hand, the hand you do not use for writing, form a circle with thumb and index finger touching. (You can use any of the fingers to touch the thumb, including the little finger. By trial and error, find the finger that works best for you.) I use the index finger. Hold it firmly against the thumb, but not as though you're fighting against or forcing an outcome.

Next, using the index finger on the opposite hand, place it inside the circle. Attempt to push the two fingers of the circle apart. Again, you are not fighting against yourself or the strength of your hand's muscles. You're allowing the muscles to determine the truth of a statement.

Strong is true. Weak is false.

Keep in mind that we're not asking questions, we're making statements that are either yes/true or no/false. If the statement is true, the muscles will remain strong and hold against the pressure. If the statement is false, the muscles will weaken and break apart as shown in the next diagram.

Critical points to remember:

- If the circle stays strong and remains as a circle, the statement is yes or true.

- If the index finger slips through the circle, the statement is no or false.

Now, practice muscle testing by making statements to which you already know the answer. In the beginning, work with only true statements.

The following is a list of examples:

- My name is _____ (use your real name).

- I am female/male. (use your correct gender)

- I live in _____ (use your correct city).

- I'm married/single. (use the correct response)

- I'm employed by _____. (Use your correct employer).

- I love/hate my job/school. (use the correct response)

- I drive a car/truck/SUV. (use the correct response)

- I have a pet/I do not have a pet. (use the correct response)

- I'm _____ years old. (use your correct age)

You get the gist of it now and can see how it works.

You already know the answers, but you practice to get a feel for the strength of the muscles in your hands. Add more true/positive statements to the list in your notebook. Work on this for several hours or even days until you feel comfortable with making positive statements.

Now, repeat the exercise above asking the same questions (along with the ones you added to your notebook) and answer them with false answers. When testing false statements, the index finger of your opposite hand should easily slip through the circle. Practice often until you're completely comfortable with the muscle testing technique. Change it up and ask many and various questions you know to be and true and you know to be false.

For example, if you name is Susan change it to my name is David or some other name that isn't yours. This gives you a complete picture of how the muscles will be weakened by a false statement or lie.

Note: Sometimes, you will get a false answer to a true statement. If this happens, you are out of balance or nervous/anxious. To correct that state of being, visualize a beam of white light running from the top of your head, down your spine, out your tailbone, and into the earth. This will balance you. You might want to incorporate that visualization in your daily rituals and routines each morning when you surround yourself with protection. If you have trouble visualizing or understanding the above directions, refer to *A Beginner's Guide to Visualization: Tips to See Clearly* by Chariss K. Walker [2018, ISBN: 978-1986634397].

Practice makes perfect.

The next section teaches you how to test using your body. If you are in public, you might not want to use the hand method or draw attention to yourself. You could use the following body method which is less noticeable.

Muscle Test Using the Body

Muscle Testing with the Sway Test Technique

"No" Response   "Yes" Response

Stand with feet firmly planted, hands by your side. Make a statement. If the answer is no or false, your body will sway backwards. If the statement is true or yes, your body will sway forwards.

Why do we need to muscle test? I've found it instrumental in my self-healing process. For example, I muscle tested the truth of the following statements:

- I should avoid grains in my diet: Yes/<u>No</u>

- Milk is harmful to my digestive system: Yes/<u>No</u>

- I have a skin disorder: <u>Yes</u>/No

- I should eliminate coffee: Yes/<u>No</u>

Some of the answers are false while some are true. Sometimes we need more clarity, for example, when I receive a 'no/false' response to the above coffee statement, I took it a step further using different variables as you can see below by my underlined answers. You will want to experiment with the method as I did.

- It's all right to drink five cups of coffee each day: <u>Yes</u>/No

- Five cups of coffee each day is too much caffeine for me: Yes/<u>No</u>

- Coffee is good for me: <u>Yes</u>/No

- Coffee is not good for me: Yes/<u>No</u>

- Black coffee is best for me: <u>Yes</u>/No

- Coffee with cream and sugar is best for me: Yes/<u>No</u>

Muscle testing opens an entirely new world to you. Ever wonder which supplement to buy in the health section of your local store? Ever wonder which bread to buy? Ever wonder which yogurt is best for you? There are so many choices, right? Point to one and test for a response.

Again, use caution. You are allowed to test your own circumstances and situations. You are not allowed to test other people unless you are granted permission. Don't be that person who "knows it all." Just because that supplement is the one best for you, doesn't mean it is best for your sister or friend. Nor should you attempt to instruct anyone on what is best for them.

In summary, by making those previous statements about coffee, I received positive answers to the following statements: coffee is good for me, black coffee is best for me, and it is all right to drink five cups of coffee each day. Next time I was at the grocery store, I pointed to different brands of coffee while making a positive statement:

- This is the best brand of coffee for me: Yes/No

Your Notes:

Your Notes:

<u>Your Notes:</u>

Your Notes:

Your Notes:

Your Notes:

Your Notes:

Your Notes:

2 | Digging-up Trapped Emotions, A Simple Method

The oldest and strongest emotion of mankind is fear, and the oldest and strongest kind of fear is fear of the unknown. ~~ H. P. Lovecraft

Please read this entire chapter before you begin to work on your releases. There are many ways to release trapped emotions (TEs). Some methods are listed below:

- Use a magnet to pull out the TEs
- Use the chakra in the palm of right hand to pull out the TEs
- Visualize that the TEs exit the top of your head into a chimney flue
- Visualize a vacuum cleaner sucking out the TEs
- Dig-up TEs using my method
- And more...

With any of the release techniques, you are required to visualize or imagine the release of the TEs. If you need help learning visualization, please see my book, *A Beginner's Guide to*

Visualization: Tips to See Clearly by Chariss K. Walker, [2018, ISBN: 978-1986634397].

As I allowed the Universe to teach me about my personal trapped emotions, I found that my thoughts returned to the days of childhood where my father was a farmer and my mother always grew a vegetable garden. Many images of his toiling to raise a thousand acres of soybeans and her struggle to raise fresh vegetables came back to me. I discovered that trapped emotions had stubborn and persistent layers. Some refer to these as heart walls, but to me, it seemed that the stubborn trapped emotions were seedbeds.

A seedbed is a bed of soil where seedlings or young plants are germinated or allowed to grow from a seed into a new individual plant. At the end of the growing season, the soil must be turned again, plowed under, and all the debris of the past growth is left behind to compost. But sometimes, it doesn't compost – it sits there and is always there.

Past growth can include:

- old seeds
- roots
- stems
- pieces

When I released my personal trapped emotions, I found relief within one to three days, but sometimes the condition didn't completely go away. I meditated on this and found that those stubborn trapped emotions were what were left behind – the debris of past growth such as emotionally charged events, thoughts, hurts, and pains. My stubborn trapped emotions were buried deeply within the soil. That soil or seedbed was filled with old seeds, roots, stems, and pieces of those events that had never composted or disintegrated. They had not become organic matter to enrich the soil – they remained a burdensome, broken mess that needed some TLC.

It was through that understanding that I developed my own technique of releasing trapped emotions (TEs). It is a simple method that works for me and I know it will work for you.

Digging-Up Trapped Emotions (TEs) Method

1. I pay special attention to my body, my mind, and my overall well-being. I notice if anything seems to be causing me difficulty. I use one of several lists of specific items (whether emotional, physical, or limitations, etc.) to determine and identify my specific trapped emotions.
2. I muscle test the list for the TEs I have and record them in my notebook.
3. I muscle test the TEs found to determine which one I should release first and list them in order or number them.
4. I muscle test each TE to determine if there are seedbeds (the stubborn ones) by making the following statement: These TEs have seedbeds: Yes/No
5. If 'yes,' I visualize the size of the seedbed. Is it 3' x 3'? Or is it larger? Smaller?
6. If 'no,' I visualize the location of the TE. If I don't know the location, I visualize a plant to represent the TE.
7. I test for which tool I need to use to dig-up the TEs: trowel, hoe, garden plow, or farming plow.
8. Depending on my answer, I visualize that my plow, big or small, is digging up all the trapped emotions. If digging up a seedbed, I see the plow covering every inch and corner of that area. If it is not a seedbed, I visualize the area in my body. If I do not know the location, I visualize a dried plant that should be pulled up and tossed in the compost pile. Then, I work on digging up the earth where that plant was removed, making sure to dig-up the roots and any pieces that might remain after pulling up the dried plant.
9. After digging for a few moments, I make the statement: My TEs of _____ are All Clear: Yes/No

10. If the answer is negative or 'No,' I continue to digging until the answer is positive or 'Yes.' Warning: this can sometimes continue for many sessions. Don't give up. Keep detailed records and continue to work on the TE release until your response to the 'All Clear' statement is 'Yes.' Don't move to release the next TE until that one is All Clear.
11. After releasing all TEs in seedbeds, I visualize that the soil is turned and I can see the old seeds, roots, stems, and pieces of the previous TEs.
12. Then, I visualize a blow torch in my hands as I move across the seedbed and burn off all the final debris such as seeds, roots, stems, and pieces until they are all gone and turned to ash. (You can use any method to burn off these TEs such as a can of gasoline and a book of matches. Use your imagination and what feels right to you.)
13. Finally, I make this statement: "I bless this seedbed with love and light so that anything that grows there again only grows from seeds of light." If you don't want to make that particular statement, use your own.

Special Note: Never begin a new release until you have completed the one you're working on.

Keep in mind that you can dig-up TEs while doing any number of things: washing dishes, cleaning, watching television, surfing the internet, taking a walk, scrolling through your text messages, or almost anything else that doesn't require your full attention. I wouldn't suggest that you do your releases while driving or operating heavy equipment of course. But still, you can multi-task. I do this especially for those TEs that seem to require a lot of digging-up.

For those of you who are not familiar with farming equipment, you will find pictures of different kinds of plows below. The trowel, hoe, and simple garden plow are used for small gardening projects while the other large plow is used by farmers and pulled by a tractor or other piece of heavy equipment for commercial farming endeavors. You will muscle test in order to decide which you should use to dig up your own trapped emotions (TEs).

"Intention" is paramount in all spiritual work. And, this is spiritual or metaphysical work.

Simple garden trowel:

Simple garden hoe:

Simple garden plow:

Large Farming plow:

Each time you begin to do a release for a particular TE, muscle test to determine which tool would be more beneficial. Once you have found the appropriate tool for the TEs you are releasing there isn't a need to keep checking until you are ready to release a new TE.

To determine which tool is most beneficial, make the following statements:

To release my TEs, I need to use the trowel: Yes/No

To release my TEs, I need to use the hoe: Yes/No

To release my TEs, I need to use the garden plow: Yes/No

To release my TEs, I need to use the large farming plow: Yes/No

Here's an example of a recent release I did. After noticing a red rash breakout on my back, I knew that something had changed. Wanting to find and release those TEs, I first asked the following questions and underlined my answer:

I have TEs in my skin system: **Yes**/No

I have TEs in my skin system organs: Yes/**No**

I have TEs in my skin system areas: Yes/**No**

I have TEs in my skin system functions: **Yes**/No

Then, I determined that I needed to use the garden plow and checked each of the skin system functions until I found the TEs I had. I wrote them in my release notebook:

- The function of new cell growth
- The function that causes red rashes

Next, I visualized, imagined, saw in my mind's eye the garden plow dig, and dig, and dig to release those TEs. I muscle tested every couple of minutes, making the following statements:

My TEs in the function of new cell growth are released: Yes/No

When the answer was 'No,' I continued to visualize the plow digging up those TEs until the answer was 'Yes." Then I made a final statement:

My TEs in the function of new cell growth is All Clear: Yes/No

When all the TEs were gone, I got a positive or 'Yes' answer to the All Clear statement. I repeated the release for TEs that cause red rashes.

If you have many TEs as I did in the beginning when I first began to release TEs, this can be an enormous task and it can take a while. Be patient because it is well worth the effort and... If you will stay with it you will see results within one to three days (sometimes a bit longer) of each release... Releasing your TEs only gets better as you release more TEs and as time passes.

As an effort to keep you from becoming discouraged, I will share a miserable experience I had releasing TEs about a hip problem I once had. First, it was very painful. Second, I lost mobility. I could not pick my leg up and step forward. I had to put my hand under my hip joint and lift my leg to walk. It hurt to sit, to recline, or to move. I could only get comfortable when lying flat on my back in bed with my right leg elevated slightly. It was a sharp pain, but it also felt deep inside. The problem happened overnight. I didn't feel it coming on and begin my release before the pain became terrible, because I didn't have any warning. By the time I started the release of my TEs causing that hip problem and pain, it was full blown and critical.

As a healer, I knew that something was out of balance in my life. The hips carry the body forward in any situation. When there are hip problems, it signifies that we don't like the forward step we have just taken or that we are fearful about moving forward in a particular direction. That fit me perfectly because I had just moved to a new state and I didn't like it... but I was too stubborn to admit it. I felt out of sorts and didn't know what to do about it. I really wanted to move back to North Carolina, but I tried to force myself to give the new area some time and not be hasty about making the decision to tuck and run back to a safety net.

Since I couldn't sit at my desk to either write or promote the books I'd already written, I worked exclusively on releasing those TEs that had caused such pain and turmoil in my life. I released TEs day and night for three weeks. True, it took a very long time, but gradually the pain receded and I was able to sit in the car for eight to ten hours a day and make the two-day trip back home even though the TEs were not completely released.

After I returned to what I felt was my safety net, I continued to work on those TEs until I received an All Clear. Several weeks later, I could walk again without the use of a cane. A few weeks later, I could once again go up and down stairs. A year later, I was better than ever.

You can see that releasing your TEs could be an overwhelming task like that instance I described. But, if you are persistent and determined, you will achieve success.

Your Notes:

Your Notes:

Your Notes:

Your Notes:

Your Notes:

3 | Universal Human Emotions

Human behavior flows from three main sources: desire, emotion, and knowledge. ~ Plato

All sentient life, all and everything that is capable of feeling and perception and responds to those feelings emotionally, have common emotions. In my research for writing this book, I found many online definitions of 'emotions' and share those definitions below.

What are emotions and what does it mean to be emotional?

- Emotions are feelings that we have about someone or something.
- Emotions are often heightened feelings meaning that we feel strongly about the person or thing.
- Emotions are a natural instinctive state of mind derived from one's circumstances, mood, or relationships with others; a feeling or sentiment.
- Emotions are an instinctive or intuitive feeling as distinguished from reasoning or knowledge.
- Emotions are the affective aspect of consciousness, a state of feeling, a conscious mental reaction such as anger or fear subjectively experienced as strong feeling usually directed toward a specific object and typically accompanied by physiological and behavioral changes in the body.

- Emotions are an affective state of consciousness in which joy, sorrow, fear, hate, or the like, is experienced, as distinguished from cognitive and volitional states of consciousness.

We share the same emotions; everyone, everywhere is capable of feeling any of these common emotions. We hope to stay positive, to feel all those emotions listed in the following positive emotions list, but sometimes we simply feel negative emotions. Sometimes those negative emotions rule our lives and cause tremendous damage to us, our relationships, our health, and our spirit.

This book does not intend to state that all emotions are wrong and should be erased. We need to feel our emotions. This book is intended to release harmful emotions that affect our lives and hinder our success whether personal, professional, or spiritual.

Never be ashamed of what you feel. You have the right to feel any emotion that you want, and to do what makes you happy. That's my life motto. ~ Demi Lovato

I have divided the most common human or universal emotions into three lists: positive, negative, and both. Think about each one carefully as you read through the lists. Perhaps you can think of more. If so, please add them to your notebook.

Positive Emotions:

- Acceptance
- Adoration
- Affection
- Amusement
- Amazement
- Anticipation
- Arousal
- Astonishment
- Attraction
- Bliss
- Caring
- Compassion
- Confusion
- Courage
- Delight
- Desire
- Ecstasy
- Elation
- Empathy
- Enthusiasm
- Euphoria
- Excitement
- Exhilaration
- Fondness
- Forgiveness
- Gaiety
- Gratitude
- Happiness
- Hope
- Infatuation
- Interest
- Joy

- Jubilation
- Kindness
- Love
- Modesty
- Patience
- Pity
- Pleasure
- Sentimentality
- Shyness
- Surprise
- Sympathy
- Trust

Negative Emotions:

- Agitation
- Aggravation
- Aggression
- Alarm
- Alienation
- Ambivalence
- Anger
- Anxiety
- Apathy
- Arousal
- Bitterness
- Confusion
- Contempt
- Cruelty
- Dejection
- Depression
- Despair

- Disdain
- Disgust
- Distress
- Doubt
- Envy
- Fear
- Fright
- Frustration
- Fury
- Greed
- Grief
- Grouchiness
- Guilt
- Hate
- Hatred
- Helplessness
- Horror
- Hostility
- Hunger
- Humiliation
- Hysteria
- Indignation
- Insecurity
- Jealousy
- Loathing
- Loneliness
- Lust
- Mortification
- Obsession
- Over-trusting
- Panic
- Paranoia
- Pride
- Rage

- Regret
- Remorse
- Resentment
- Revulsion
- Shame
- Suffering
- Tension
- Thrill
- Worry
- Wrath

Shame is the most powerful master emotion. It's the fear that we're not good enough.
~~ Brene Brown

Both Positive and Negative Emotions:

- Ambivalence
- Arousal
- Boredom
- Embarrassment
- Homesickness
- Passion
- Sadness
- Trust

When dealing with people, remember you are not dealing with creatures of logic, but creatures of emotion. ~~ Dale Carnegie

Your Notes:

Your Notes:

Your Notes:

Your Notes:

Your Notes:

Your Notes:

4 | A Look at Positive Emotions

Although we won't be releasing positive emotions, we will look at this list and make some statements about each one. Joy and happiness are wonderful emotions; however, we must consider that we can have TEs that prevent joy or happiness. Read through the following statements for a full understanding of how our positive emotions might need some work. As you begin to muscle test the statements, please notate your answers in your notebook. Make a complete list of any TEs that you have before you begin to release them.

With that in mind, we will make the following statements to discover any TEs:

- I have TEs that prevent me from feeling Acceptance: Yes/No
- I have TEs that prevent me from feeling Adoration: Yes/No
- I have TEs that prevent me from feeling Affection: Yes/No
- I have TEs that prevent me from feeling Amusement: Yes/No
- I have TEs that prevent me from feeling Amazement: Yes/No
- I have TEs that prevent me from feeling Anticipation: Yes/No

- I have TEs that prevent me from feeling Arousal: Yes/No
- I have TEs that prevent me from feeling Astonishment: Yes/No
- I have TEs that prevent me from feeling Attraction: Yes/No
- I have TEs that prevent me from feeling Bliss: Yes/No
- I have TEs that prevent me from feeling Caring: Yes/No
- I have TEs that prevent me from feeling Compassion: Yes/No
- I have TEs that prevent me from feeling Courage: Yes/No
- I have TEs that prevent me from feeling Delight: Yes/No
- I have TEs that prevent me from feeling Desire: Yes/No
- I have TEs that prevent me from feeling Ecstasy: Yes/No
- I have TEs that prevent me from feeling Elation: Yes/No
- I have TEs that prevent me from feeling Empathy: Yes/No
- I have TEs that prevent me from feeling Enthusiasm: Yes/No
- I have TEs that prevent me from feeling Euphoria: Yes/No
- I have TEs that prevent me from feeling Excitement: Yes/No
- I have TEs that prevent me from feeling Exhilaration: Yes/No
- I have TEs that prevent me from feeling Fondness: Yes/No
- I have TEs that prevent me from feeling Forgiveness: Yes/No
- I have TEs that prevent me from feeling Gaiety: Yes/No
- I have TEs that prevent me from feeling Happiness: Yes/No

- I have TEs that prevent me from feeling Hope: Yes/No
- I have TEs that prevent me from feeling Infatuation: Yes/No
- I have TEs that prevent me from feeling Interest: Yes/No
- I have TEs that prevent me from feeling Joy: Yes/No
- I have TEs that prevent me from feeling Jubilation: Yes/No
- I have TEs that prevent me from feeling Kindness: Yes/No
- I have TEs that prevent me from feeling Love: Yes/No
- I have TEs that prevent me from feeling Modesty: Yes/No
- I have TEs that prevent me from feeling Patience: Yes/No
- I have TEs that prevent me from feeling Pity: Yes/No
- I have TEs that prevent me from feeling Pleasure: Yes/No
- I have TEs that prevent me from feeling Sentimentality: Yes/No
- I have TEs that prevent me from feeling Shyness: Yes/No
- I have TEs that prevent me from feeling Surprise: Yes/No
- I have TEs that prevent me from feeling Sympathy: Yes/No
- I have TEs that prevent me from feeling Trust: Yes/No

Record each 'Yes' in your notebook or the space provided.

Next, muscle test to determine which one you should release first.

Number each TE in order of first to last before you begin the release.

Special Note: Never begin a new release until you have completed the one working on.

What's next? Once we have arranged our list in the preferred order of release, we release those TEs. As an example for you to follow, this is how I proceed:

1. I muscle test each TE to determine if there are seedbeds (the stubborn ones) by making the following statement: These TEs have seedbeds: Yes/No
2. If 'yes,' I visualize the size of the seedbed. Is it 3' x 3'? Is it larger? Smaller?
3. If there aren't any seedbeds, I visualize the location of the TE. If I don't know the location, I visualize a dried plant to represent the TE.
4. I test for which tool I need to use to dig-up the TEs: trowel, hoe, garden plow, or farming plow.
5. Depending on my answer, I visualize that my plow, big or small, is digging up all the trapped emotions. If digging up a seedbed, I see the plow covering every inch and corner of that area. If it is not a seedbed, I visualize the area in my body. If I do not know the location, I visualize a dried plant that should be pulled up and tossed in the compost pile. Then, I work on digging up the earth where that plant was removed, making sure to dig-up the roots and any pieces that might remain after pulling up the dried plant, even those pesky little spidery roots.
6. After digging for a few moments, I make the statement: My TEs of _____ are All Clear: Yes/No
7. If the answer is negative or 'No,' I continue to digging until the answer is positive or 'Yes.' I warn you now that

this can sometimes continue for many sessions. Don't give up and don't move to a new TE until you have completed this one. Keep detailed records and continue to work on the TE release until your response to the 'All Clear' statement is 'Yes.'

8. After releasing all TEs in seedbeds, I visualize that the soil is finely turned and I can see the old seeds, roots, stems, and pieces of the previous TEs.

9. Then, I visualize a blow torch in my hands as I move across the seedbed and burn off all the final debris such as seeds, roots, stems, and pieces until they are all gone and turned to ash. (You can use any method to burn off these TEs such as a can of gasoline and a book of matches.)

10. Finally, I make this statement: "I bless this seedbed with love and light so that anything that grows there again only grows from seeds of light." If you don't want to make that particular statement, use your own.

Repeat for each TE found. Keep detailed notes.

Your Notes:

<u>Your Notes:</u>

<u>Your Notes:</u>

Your Notes:

Your Notes:

Your Notes:

Your Notes:

Your Notes:

5 | A Look at Negative Emotions

It seems that negative emotions are often the bane of our existence. We fight the emotion of envy or jealousy, but it always seems to return. With that in mind, and because we want to release those trapped emotions, we will make the following statements:

- I have TEs that cause me to feel excessive Agitation: Yes/No
- I have TEs that cause me to feel excessive Aggravation: Yes/No
- I have TEs that cause me to feel excessive Aggression: Yes/No
- I have TEs that cause me to feel excessive Alarm: Yes/No
- I have TEs that cause me to feel excessive Alienation: Yes/No
- I have TEs that cause me to feel excessive Ambivalence: Yes/No
- I have TEs that cause me to feel excessive Anger: Yes/No
- I have TEs that cause me to feel excessive Anxiety: Yes/No
- I have TEs that cause me to feel excessive Apathy: Yes/No
- I have TEs that cause me to feel excessive Arousal: Yes/No
- I have TEs that cause me to feel excessive Bitterness: Yes/No
- I have TEs that cause me to feel excessive Confusion: Yes/No
- I have TEs that cause me to feel excessive Contempt: Yes/No
- I have TEs that cause me to feel excessive Cruelty: Yes/No

- I have TEs that cause me to feel excessive Dejection: Yes/No
- I have TEs that cause me to feel excessive Depression: Yes/No
- I have TEs that cause me to feel excessive Despair: Yes/No
- I have TEs that cause me to feel excessive Disdain: Yes/No
- I have TEs that cause me to feel excessive Disgust: Yes/No
- I have TEs that cause me to feel excessive Distress: Yes/No
- I have TEs that cause me to feel excessive Doubt: Yes/No
- I have TEs that cause me to feel excessive Envy: Yes/No
- I have TEs that cause me to feel excessive Fear: Yes/No
- I have TEs that cause me to feel excessive Fright: Yes/No
- I have TEs that cause me to feel excessive Frustration: Yes/No
- I have TEs that cause me to feel excessive Fury: Yes/No
- I have TEs that cause me to feel excessive Grief: Yes/No
- I have TEs that cause me to feel excessive Grouchiness: Yes/No
- I have TEs that cause me to feel excessive Guilt: Yes/No
- I have TEs that cause me to feel excessive Hate: Yes/No
- I have TEs that cause me to feel excessive Hatred: Yes/No
- I have TEs that cause me to feel excessive Helplessness: Yes/No
- I have TEs that cause me to feel excessive Horror: Yes/No
- I have TEs that cause me to feel excessive Hostility: Yes/No
- I have TEs that cause me to feel excessive Hunger: Yes/No
- I have TEs that cause me to feel excessive Humiliation: Yes/No
- I have TEs that cause me to feel excessive Hysteria: Yes/No
- I have TEs that cause me to feel excessive Indignation: Yes/No
- I have TEs that cause me to feel excessive Insecurity: Yes/No
- I have TEs that cause me to feel excessive Jealousy: Yes/No
- I have TEs that cause me to feel excessive Loathing: Yes/No

- I have TEs that cause me to feel excessive Loneliness: Yes/No
- I have TEs that cause me to feel excessive Lust: Yes/No
- I have TEs that cause me to feel excessive Mortification: Yes/No
- I have TEs that cause me to feel excessive Obsession: Yes/No
- I have TEs that cause me to feel excessive Over-trusting: Yes/No
- I have TEs that cause me to feel excessive Panic: Yes/No
- I have TEs that cause me to feel excessive Paranoia: Yes/No
- I have TEs that cause me to feel excessive Pride: Yes/No
- I have TEs that cause me to feel excessive Rage: Yes/No
- I have TEs that cause me to feel excessive Regret: Yes/No
- I have TEs that cause me to feel excessive Remorse: Yes/No
- I have TEs that cause me to feel excessive Resentment: Yes/No
- I have TEs that cause me to feel excessive Revulsion: Yes/No
- I have TEs that cause me to feel excessive Shame: Yes/No
- I have TEs that cause me to feel excessive Sorrow: Yes/No
- I have TEs that cause me to feel excessive Suffering: Yes/No
- I have TEs that cause me to feel excessive Tension: Yes/No
- I have TEs that cause me to feel excessive Thrill: Yes/No
- I have TEs that cause me to feel excessive Worry: Yes/No

Record each 'Yes' in your notebook or the space provided.

Next, muscle test to determine which one you should release first.

Number each TE in order of first to last before you begin the release.

Special Note: Never begin a new release until you have completed the one working on.

Once we have arranged our list in the preferred order of release, we release those TEs. As an example for you to follow, this is how I proceed:

1. I muscle test each TE to determine if there are seedbeds (the stubborn ones) by making the following statement: These TEs have seedbeds: Yes/No
2. If 'yes,' I visualize the size of the seedbed. Is it 3' x 3'? Is it larger? Smaller?
3. If there aren't any seedbeds, I visualize the location of the TE. If I don't know the location, I visualize a dried plant to represent the TE.
4. I test for which tool I need to use to dig-up the TEs: trowel, hoe, garden plow, or farming plow.
5. Depending on my answer, I visualize that my plow, big or small, is digging up all the trapped emotions. If digging up a seedbed, I see the plow covering every inch and corner of that area. If it is not a seedbed, I visualize the area in my body. If I do not know the location, I visualize a dried plant that should be pulled up and tossed in the compost pile. Then, I work on digging up the earth where that plant was removed, making sure to dig-up the roots and any pieces that might remain after pulling up the dried plant, even those pesky little spidery roots.
6. After digging for a few moments, I make the statement: My TEs of _____ are All Clear: Yes/No
7. If the answer is negative or 'No,' I continue to digging until the answer is positive or 'Yes.' I warn you now that this can sometimes continue for many sessions. Don't give up and don't move to a new TE until you have completed this one. Keep detailed records and continue to work on the TE release until your response to the 'All Clear' statement is 'Yes.'

8. After releasing all TEs in seedbeds, I visualize that the soil is finely turned and I can see the old seeds, roots, stems, and pieces of the previous TEs.
9. Then, I visualize a blow torch in my hands as I move across the seedbed and burn off all the final debris such as seeds, roots, stems, and pieces until they are all gone and turned to ash. (You can use any method to burn off these TEs such as a can of gasoline and a book of matches.)
10. Finally, I make this statement: "I bless this seedbed with love and light so that anything that grows there again only grows from seeds of light." If you don't want to make that particular statement, use your own.

Repeat for each TE found. Keep detailed notes.

Your Notes:

<u>Your Notes:</u>

Your Notes:

Your Notes:

Your Notes:

Your Notes:

Your Notes:

Your Notes:

6 | A Look at Both Positive and Negative Emotions

Sometimes emotions are neither good nor bad, they simply are there, and unfortunately they can cause trouble in our mind, body, or soul. With that in mind, we will test to see if we have any of these neutral trapped emotions.

Make the following statements:

I have TEs that cause me to feel excessive Ambivalence: Yes/No

I have TEs that cause me to feel excessive Boredom: Yes/No

I have TEs that cause me to feel excessive Embarrassment: Yes/No

I have TEs that cause me to feel excessive Homesickness: Yes/No

I have TEs that cause me to feel excessive longing: Yes/No

I have TEs that cause me to feel excessive Passion: Yes/No

I have TEs that cause me to feel excessive Sadness: Yes/No

I have TEs that cause me to feel excessive Trust: Yes/No

Record each 'Yes' in your notebook or the space provided.

Next, muscle test to determine which one you should release first.

Number each TE in order of first to last before you begin the release.

Special Note: Never begin a new release until you have completed the one working on.

Once we have arranged our list in the preferred order of release, we release those TEs. As an example for you to follow, this is how I proceed:

1. I muscle test each TE to determine if there are seedbeds (the stubborn ones) by making the following statement: These TEs have seedbeds: Yes/No
2. If 'yes,' I visualize the size of the seedbed. Is it 3' x 3'? Is it larger? Smaller?
3. If there aren't any seedbeds, I visualize the location of the TE. If I don't know the location, I visualize a dried plant to represent the TE.
4. I test for which tool I need to use to dig-up the TEs: trowel, hoe, garden plow, or farming plow.
5. Depending on my answer, I visualize that my plow, big or small, is digging up all the trapped emotions. If digging up a seedbed, I see the plow covering every inch and corner of that area. If it is not a seedbed, I visualize the area in my body. If I do not know the location, I visualize a dried plant that should be pulled up and tossed in the compost pile. Then, I work on digging up the earth where that plant was removed, making sure to dig-up the roots and any pieces that might remain after pulling up the dried plant, even those pesky little spidery roots.
6. After digging for a few moments, I make the statement: My TEs of _____ are All Clear: Yes/No

7. If the answer is negative or 'No,' I continue to digging until the answer is positive or 'Yes.' I warn you now that this can sometimes continue for many sessions. Don't give up and don't move to a new TE until you have completed this one. Keep detailed records and continue to work on the TE release until your response to the 'All Clear' statement is 'Yes.'

8. After releasing all TEs in seedbeds, I visualize that the soil is finely turned and I can see the old seeds, roots, stems, and pieces of the previous TEs.

9. Then, I visualize a blow torch in my hands as I move across the seedbed and burn off all the final debris such as seeds, roots, stems, and pieces until they are all gone and turned to ash. (You can use any method to burn off these TEs such as a can of gasoline and a book of matches.)

10. Finally, I make this statement: "I bless this seedbed with love and light so that anything that grows there again only grows from seeds of light." If you don't want to make that particular statement, use your own.

Repeat for each TE found. Keep detailed notes.

Your Notes

Your Notes:

Your Notes:

<u>Your Notes:</u>

Your Notes:

Your Notes:

Your Notes:

Your Notes:

7 | Tips to Release More Trapped Emotions

The previous chapters have gotten you started, but there might be other areas where you have emotional TEs. Go back through each list of the positive, negative, and both lists of emotions. Think about each carefully. Perhaps as you mediate on each emotion, something will come to mind that is a troubling area in your life.

For example, under the list for positive emotions, you might change the wording to make other statements such as these:

I have TEs that prevent me from feeling acceptance at work: Yes/No

I have TEs that prevent me from feeling acceptance in my profession: Yes/No

I have TEs that prevent me from feeling acceptance in my family: Yes/No

I have TEs that prevent me from feeling acceptance in my immediate family: Yes/No

I have TEs that prevent me from feeling acceptance in my extended family: Yes/No

I have TEs that prevent me from feeling acceptance in my paternal family: Yes/No

I have TEs that prevent me from feeling acceptance in my maternal family: Yes/No

I have TEs that prevent me from feeling acceptance in social settings: Yes/No

I have TEs that prevent me from feeling acceptance with coworkers: Yes/No

I have TEs that prevent me from feeling acceptance in family social settings: Yes/No

I have TEs that prevent me from feeling acceptance in my romantic relationship: Yes/No

I have TEs that prevent me from feeling self-acceptance: Yes/No

I have TEs that prevent me from feeling that the world accepts me: Yes/No

You can now understand how many ways you can make the acceptance statement to fit a particular area of your specific life, especially when you know of those specific areas that are troubling.

In your notebook, go back through the list. Make notes about each statement that gives you pause or causes even the slightest emotional inkling that there is more in regards to that TE. Then, dissect it; make it the exact statement that fits your situation perfectly.

Repeat this process for Positive Emotions, Negative Emotions, and Both Emotions.

Keep detailed notes, then release all the TEs that you have found using the previously described digging technique.

You have now released your Emotional TEs. I suggest that you revisit your notebook again in a few months. Recheck each previous TE you have listed. If you get any 'Yes' answers to your statements, release those TEs right away. It doesn't happen often, but it can happen because even though we have released the TEs, we might not have changed the pattern in our lives that caused the TE.

Be sure to continue your self-healing discovery by reading and working through the other books in this series.

Your Notes:

Your Notes:

Your Notes:

Your Notes:

Your Notes:

<u>Your Notes:</u>

<u>Your Notes:</u>

Your Notes:

You may continue with any other books in the *Going Deeper* series.

A Beginner's Guide to Releasing Trapped Emotions (Going Deeper, Book 1)

Release Chakra Trapped Emotions (Going Deeper, Book 2)

Release Common Disease Trapped Emotions (Going Deeper, Book 3)

Release Hindrances to Success, (Going Deeper, Book 4)

Release Body System Trapped Emotions, (Going Deeper, Book 5)

Release Mental Blocks, (Going Deeper, Book 6)

Thank you for reading this book. If you enjoyed the book, please leave a few words or sentences as a review. A review means a lot to every author and it lets others know the book's value. I know reviews are very important to me. Just a simple, "I liked it" or "I learned something from this book" is greatly appreciated.

Keep reading for an excerpt from *A Beginner's Guide to Visualization: Tips to See Clearly.*

<u>Your Notes:</u>

A Beginner's Guide to Visualization:
Tips to See Clearly *Excerpt*

©2018 Chariss K. Walker

Chariss K. Walker

Introduction

A little about me and why I've written this book: I've studied metaphysical sciences along with religion and spirituality for over thirty years. I have a master's degree in Metaphysical Sciences and an honorary doctorate in Divinity, but I've also spent a lot of time forming my own opinion about these topics through experience, reading and studying what others have to say, and helping others. In spite of all this, I consider myself an average person who desires to help others by sharing all that I have learned.

 Still, with all that has been written by scholars and people who have far more degrees than I do, there seems to be a lack of basic information that would improve our lives. This concept reminds me of a friend or relative who makes a wonder chocolate cake. When asked for her recipe, she begrudgingly shares it, and in the process, leaves out one special ingredient that makes the mixture so divine. Those who make her recipe never get the same results. I don't want to be like that person. I want my readers to know what I know.

This book might feel simplistic to some, but I'm not convinced that the information I share in this text is widely known. With that in mind, I want this information to be easily understood. I promise not to get too extravagant or use words that you have to look up in order to understand the context. I'm going to write this book as simply as possible and elaborate with examples and details, including personal experiences, in hopes that anyone reading this text can understand what is within these pages. If I repeat something you already know, perhaps the next person doesn't know that information. If I repeat something I've already said, I do so in order to stress its importance.

Some books about spiritual laws, prosperity, new-age topics, and other metaphysical subjects are written by authors who haven't made the discussion easy to comprehend. Sometimes, they don't follow through with illustrations that expand the concepts. And, unfortunately, sometimes, they leave out a simple concept that would really benefit us. It is my desire to provide as much information as possible so that what I have written is easy to read and understand, not only in this book, but in all the books I author.

Special Note: If you are reading the paperback version of this book, I have left space for your notes. If you are reading the eBook version, I recommend that you have a notebook and pen available to record the exercises given as well as your thoughts and inspirations as you read. Most people learn best by reading, writing down what they've read, and then, explaining the information to another.

Chapter 1 | Understanding Visualization

To visualize is to "see something in your mind's eye" or to "imagine something." It's also to create a positive mental picture of something such as a desired outcome. When done correctly, to visualize good things happening to us promotes a sense of comfort and well-being.

Why?

Because you are acting as if those good things have already happened. You are pretending, role-playing, play-acting, that good things come from the good pictures you imagined.

To imagine a positive outcome is a very important aspect of visualization.

If we trust the concept of Universal Laws, then we must evaluate The Law of Attraction.

The Law of Attraction – Like attracts like – specifically demands that whatever we think about the most is drawn to us like a magnet.

Let's rephrase that statement to include:

- whatever we dream
- whatever creates a mental picture or image
- whatever we imagine
- whatever ideas we have

So to expand on the Law of Attraction with that in mind, that law specifically demands that whatever we think about, whatever we dream, whatever creates a mental picture, whatever ideas we have most often is drawn and attracted to us like a magnet. Those thoughts and ideas entice and encourage those dreams, images, and ideas to come to us.

Now, consider this: if we think about good things, good things will find us, right?

What good things will find us?

Does it matter as long as it is something good?

It does to me and I can only imagine that it does to you also.

Likewise, if we think about bad things, bad things will also find us, right?

But, exactly what bad things will find us?

Does that matter?

It does to me... and again, I can only imagine that it does to you as well.

Can you see the conundrum and confusion in that?

Let's take that further... If I think happy thoughts, I will feel happy and joyous.

If I think sad, depressing thoughts, I will feel sad and depressed.

I cannot think sad and happy thoughts at the same time. One will cancel out the other.

If you don't believe that previous statement, try it now. Try to think of a happy memory and then a bad memory. You will leave one memory for the other because the mind cannot entertain two opposing thoughts at the same time.

This we understand.

Now, what else is missing from our understanding?

Can we think about things other than positivity?

Can we think about other things besides joy, happiness, elation, pleasurable thought?

Can we include good material possessions or personal achievements?

Of course we can. Our thoughts can expand into any area of our body, mind, and soul because we are multidimensional beings.

We are not human beings on a spiritual journey. We are spiritual beings on a human journey.
~ **Pierre Teilhard de Chardin (1881 – 1955)**

We can visualize financial prosperity and abundance, spiritual prosperity and growth, personal health and wellness, the list is simply endless.

I like to visualize those things that bring me joy.

Certain things bring joy to me when I ponder or think about them. For example, I feel happy and content when I know I have helped someone through personal interaction or through my writings. I feel joyful when someone leaves a review about one of my books to let me know that it inspired or helped them on their personal journey.

As another example, when I think about financial or material prosperity, I feel happy when I consider helping my family, providing something special for them that they can't afford to do on their own.

I believe that the entire purpose of prosperity is to share and give to our loved ones. In my estimation, there is no joy in having anything that can't be shared.

What brings you joy?

In the space provided or in your notebook, make a list of five things that bring you joy.

<u>Your Notes:</u>

Your Notes:

Your Notes:

Your Notes:

About the Author

Chariss K Walker, M. Msc, an award-winning author, writes fiction and nonfiction books with a metaphysical message. All of her books are sold in soft-cover and eBook formats worldwide, many are in large print.

In her nonfiction books, Chariss writes to share her extensive knowledge about metaphysical concepts – those things which can't easily be explained by science such as auras, chakras, love, visions, and healing. In her fiction books, she shares a characters personal growth as he or she learns to accept their unique abilities.

To find out more about this author, visit her website @ www.chariss.com.

You can find Chariss here:

Amazon Authors

Smashwords Authors

Goodreads Authors

Facebook

Pinterest

Google +

LinkedIn

Instagram

And many other social media sites

Other books by Chariss K. Walker

Nonfiction Books:
A Beginner's Guide to Visualization
Chakra Basics
The Spiritual Gifts
Abundance
Many Paths to Healing
Keep the Faith
Make a Joyful Noise
Make a Joyful Noise Study Guide
Finding Serenity 3-Book Boxed-Set

Fiction Books:
The Vision Chronicles – Paranormal Suspense Thrillers
Kaleidoscope, Book 1
Spyglass, Book 2
Window's Pane, Book 3
Windows All Around, Book 4
Open Spaces, Book 5
Stream of Light, Book 6
Lamp's Light, Book 7
Clear Glass, Book 8

The Retreat
The Journey

Dark Fiction Books:

An Alec Winters Series – Dark Urban-Fantasy/Thrillers:

Prelude, Book 1

Crescent City, Book 2

Port City, Book 3

Harbor City, Book 4

Serena McKay Novels – Dark-Dystopian Crime Female P.I. Thrillers

Purple Kitty, Book 1

Blue Cadillac, Book 2

Yellow Scarf, Book 3 (Coming Soon!)

my name is tookie

Made in the
USA
Columbia, SC